How to use this journal

This journal is your "safe space". Think about it as the place where you can say ANYTHING with no judgment from anyone. It's a place where you can just figure stuff out. Every day write about what is going on in your world. I promise ... it will help.

Let's get started.
The first thing to do is to create your I Am Statement.

This doesn't have to be what is really going on in your life. It's just what you want to happen. Think of it as making a wish.

Example: I Am peaceful and happy now because I have a place to release my stress and problems.

Now press the two record buttons and use the below script to help you record your personalized I Am statement.
I Am _____ and _____ now because I _____ .

Is there something you can touch or look at that makes it feel more real? If so, put it in your envelope.

Journal processing written by Jamie Dicken, Design/Illustrated by Emily Jones and Colleen Ster
Published by Reflections Publishing
© 2010-11 Believe in She, © 2011 Reflections Publishing
ISBN 978-1-61660-005-1

Each day before you start writing:
1. Take 3 deep breaths
2. Listen to your recorded I Am Statement 3 times
3. Touch your special object from your envelope and then ....

Download

What's going on in your world? Did something amazing happen today? Here's your chance to celebrate! Is anything bothering you? Are you thinking about it over and over again? Let it go! This is your dumping ground. Be honest. Be real. No one will see this except for you.

Dig Deep

Name at least ONE thing that you are grateful for in your life. This is easy on a good day, but on a day that is more challenging, ask yourself what good can come out of the situation. Find one good thing. You can do it!

Dream

This is the fun part. Dream about the life you want to live. Imagine the situation or your thoughts the way you want it. Write as if it has already happened.

Draw

They say a picture is worth a thousand words. Are you the creative type that expresses yourself better with images rather than words? If so, use this opportunity to draw it. Draw the world as you see it now and then as you want it to be. It doesn't have to be perfect. Sometimes a smiley face or a heart can say it all. Let that creativity shine!

Who I Am

Throughout the pages you will see some pretty powerful words and their definitions. Try them on the way you would try on a new outfit. Say "I Am ...." and see how it feels. Is this a word that feels like you? Do you want to be more like this? Maybe try bringing this word into your "I Am" statement.

Have Fun

Think about journal writing like being allowed to scream out loud in class. Nothing about this should be hard. This is all about doing what feels right for you.

Need to get some extra energy out? Follow the Yoga Girl's instructions below on the bottom of each page for a stress relieving activity.

Download

_____
_____
_____
_____
_____
_____
_____
_____
_____
_____
_____
_____
_____
_____

Dig Deep

_____
_____
_____
_____
_____
_____
_____
_____
_____
_____
_____
_____
_____
_____

I Am Joyful

I experience the happy feeling brought on by the possibility of reaching my dreams.

Draw

Dream

_____

Do a Handstand

Any time you let your feet go over your heart you release happy endorphins.

Download

Dig Deep

I Am Peaceful

I have a quiet mind free of things that bother me, distract me, or stress me out.

Draw

Dream

_____
_____
_____
_____
_____
_____
_____
_____
_____
_____
_____
_____
_____
_____

Feel the Power

Trace the infinity under the words **Believe in She** on the back cover.
Start in the middle and then go up to the left, around up to the right,
and back to center.

Download

Dig Deep

I Am Strong

I feel my power and I am able to achieve what I want in any situation.

Draw

Dream

_____
_____
_____
_____
_____
_____
_____
_____
_____
_____
_____
_____
_____
_____

Become a Warrior!

Spread your legs wide. Bend your front knee with your toes facing forward. Your back leg is straight with your foot in line with the wall behind you. Reach your arms to opposite ends of the room.

Download

_____

Dig Deep

_____

I Am **Powerful**

I am capable of doing or accomplishing anything.

Draw

Dream

Push obstacles out of your way

Place your hands on a wall and push as if you can knock it down.
Maybe even try pushing with your shoulder or your back.

Download

Dig Deep

I Am Clear

I am free from confusion, uncertainty, and doubt.

Draw

Dream

_____
_____
_____
_____
_____
_____
_____
_____
_____
_____
_____
_____
_____
_____

Jump up and down

Clear those cobwebs from your brain.

Download

_____

Dig Deep

_____

I Am Grateful

I deeply appreciate the kindness of others and feel thankful

Draw

Dream

Bow forward

Take a deep breath in and reach for the sky. Bring your hands through your heart and fold forward with a flat back until you touch the ground.

Download

Dig Deep

I Am **Happy**

I am filled with emotions of pleasure, contentment and joy.

Draw

Dream

Laugh out loud
There is no better feeling.

Download

_____
_____
_____
_____
_____
_____
_____
_____
_____
_____
_____
_____
_____
_____

Dig Deep

_____
_____
_____
_____
_____
_____
_____
_____
_____
_____
_____
_____
_____

I Am Courageous

I have the spirit to feel confident and brave when faced with challenges.

Draw

Dream

_____
_____
_____
_____
_____
_____
_____
_____
_____
_____
_____
_____
_____
_____

Time to Fly

Lean forward, spread your arms like wings, and lift one leg.

Download

Dig Deep

I Am Creative

I have the ability to use my imagination to make new things and develop original ideas.

Draw

Dream

_____
_____
_____
_____
_____
_____
_____
_____
_____
_____
_____
_____
_____
_____
_____

Create your own Dance

Just move your body around and have fun.

Download

Dig Deep

I Am Confident

I believe in me.

Draw

Dream

_____
_____
_____
_____
_____
_____
_____
_____
_____
_____
_____
_____
_____
_____

Yell "YES"

Yell as loud as you can! Doesn't that feel good?

Download

(ruled lines)

Dig Deep

(ruled lines)

I Am Spirited

I am full of life and excited to explore the world.

Draw

Dream

Do a Cartwheel

Turn your world upside down.

Download

_____
_____
_____
_____
_____
_____
_____
_____
_____
_____
_____
_____
_____

Dig Deep

_____
_____
_____
_____
_____
_____
_____
_____
_____
_____
_____
_____
_____

I Am Fun

I bring happy energy to every situation.

Draw

Dream
_____
_____
_____
_____
_____
_____
_____
_____
_____
_____
_____
_____
_____

Spin in circles!
Wheeee!

Download

Dig Deep

I Am Respectful

I recognize and acknowledge other's sense of worth.

Draw

Dream

_____
_____
_____
_____
_____
_____
_____
_____
_____
_____
_____
_____
_____
_____

Compliment someone

Let people know that you appreciate them.

Download

_____
_____
_____
_____
_____
_____
_____
_____
_____
_____
_____
_____
_____
_____

Dig Deep

_____
_____
_____
_____
_____
_____
_____
_____
_____
_____
_____
_____

I Believe

I trust my instincts and feel confident in my truth.

Draw

Dream

Breathe deeply

Seal your lips. Take a deep breath in through your nose for a
count of 4. Hold it and then release the breath back through
your nose for a count of 5.

Download

_____
_____
_____
_____
_____
_____
_____
_____
_____
_____
_____
_____
_____
_____

Dig Deep

_____
_____
_____
_____
_____
_____
_____
_____
_____
_____
_____
_____
_____

I Am Balanced

I easily juggle my life. I experience mental and emotional
stability and approach life from a place that is calm and centered.

Draw

Dream

_____
_____
_____
_____
_____
_____
_____
_____
_____
_____
_____
_____
_____
_____

Become a Tree

Plant one foot on the ground and place the other on your leg anywhere except your knee. Place your hands in front of your heart. Grow your tree by bringing your arms over your head.

Download

_____

Dig Deep

_____

I Am Inspiring

I have a positive influence on others.

Draw

Dream

_____
_____
_____
_____
_____
_____
_____
_____
_____
_____
_____
_____
_____
_____

Give Back

How can you make a difference today?

Download

_____
_____
_____
_____
_____
_____
_____
_____
_____
_____
_____
_____
_____
_____
_____

Dig Deep

_____
_____
_____
_____
_____
_____
_____
_____
_____
_____
_____
_____
_____
_____

I Am Healthy

I experience the benefits of a balanced mind, body, and spirit.

Draw

Dream

_____
_____
_____
_____
_____
_____
_____
_____
_____
_____
_____
_____
_____

Do a Twist

Twisting from side to side helps clear any bad stuff out of your body.

Download

_____

_____

_____

_____

_____

_____

_____

_____

_____

_____

_____

_____

_____

Dig Deep

_____

_____

_____

_____

_____

_____

_____

_____

_____

_____

_____

I Am Loving

I am affectionately concerned about the well-being of others.

Draw

Dream

_____
_____
_____
_____
_____
_____
_____
_____
_____
_____
_____
_____
_____

Give a Hug

Feel the love.

Download

Dig Deep

I Am Free

I clear all obstacles to live the life I want to live.

Draw

Dream

_____
_____
_____
_____
_____
_____
_____
_____
_____
_____
_____
_____

Take a Walk

Then rest and enjoy being outside breathing in the fresh air.

Download

_____
_____
_____
_____
_____
_____
_____
_____
_____
_____
_____
_____
_____

Dig Deep

_____
_____
_____
_____
_____
_____
_____
_____
_____
_____
_____
_____
_____

I Am Intentional

I create my actions and desired results.

Draw

Dream

_____
_____
_____
_____
_____
_____
_____
_____
_____
_____
_____
_____
_____

Set a Goal

What can you accomplish by the end of the month?

Download

Dig Deep

I Am Calm

I approach situations from a place that is relaxed and content.

Draw

Dream

_____
_____
_____
_____
_____
_____
_____
_____
_____
_____
_____
_____

Feel the calming Vibration

Sit down cross legged with your hands on your knees. Close
your eyes. Say the word "OM". It sounds like a - oh - um.

Download

_____
_____
_____
_____
_____
_____
_____
_____
_____
_____
_____
_____
_____

Dig Deep

_____
_____
_____
_____
_____
_____
_____
_____
_____
_____
_____
_____
_____
_____
_____
_____

I Am Centered

I am emotionally stable and secure.

Draw

Dream

_____
_____
_____
_____
_____
_____
_____
_____
_____
_____
_____
_____
_____
_____

Become a Mountain

Stand up straight with your feet together. Reach your arms up
overhead and feel your whole body come into alignment.

Download

_____
_____
_____
_____
_____
_____
_____
_____
_____
_____
_____
_____
_____
_____
_____

Dig Deep

_____
_____
_____
_____
_____
_____
_____
_____
_____
_____
_____
_____
_____
_____

I Am Connected

I am united with those around me. I have amazing relationships.

Draw

Dream

_____
_____
_____
_____
_____
_____
_____
_____
_____
_____
_____
_____
_____

Call a friend

Let them know how awesome you think they are.

Download

_____
_____
_____
_____
_____
_____
_____
_____
_____
_____
_____
_____
_____

Dig Deep

_____
_____
_____
_____
_____
_____
_____
_____
_____
_____
_____
_____
_____

I Am Empowered

I believe in me and my ability to influence others.

Draw

Dream

_____
_____
_____
_____
_____
_____
_____
_____
_____
_____
_____
_____
_____
_____

Make up your own yoga Pose

Why not?

Download

Dig Deep

I Am Intelligent

I understand things easily and use good judgment.

Draw

Dream

Look up a new **Word**

Pull out the dictionary and find something new to say.

Download

_____
_____
_____
_____
_____
_____
_____
_____
_____
_____
_____
_____
_____
_____
_____

Dig Deep

_____
_____
_____
_____
_____
_____
_____
_____
_____
_____
_____
_____
_____

I Am Compassionate

I feel sympathetic toward other people and desire to help make things better.

Draw

Dream

_____
_____
_____
_____
_____
_____
_____
_____
_____
_____
_____
_____
_____
_____

Do a **B**ackbend

Open your heart.

Download

_____
_____
_____
_____
_____
_____
_____
_____
_____
_____
_____
_____
_____
_____

Dig Deep

_____
_____
_____
_____
_____
_____
_____
_____
_____
_____
_____
_____

I Am Talented

I have the ability to achieve and experience success.

Draw

Dream

_____
_____
_____
_____
_____
_____
_____
_____
_____
_____
_____
_____
_____

Practice something you love

Show the world what you can do.

Download

_____

_____

_____

_____

_____

_____

_____

_____

_____

_____

_____

_____

_____

_____

Dig Deep

_____

_____

_____

_____

_____

_____

_____

_____

_____

_____

_____

_____

_____

_____

I Am Focused

I can concentrate my attention and effort on the task at hand.

Draw

Dream

_____
_____
_____
_____
_____
_____
_____
_____
_____
_____
_____
_____

Center your energy

Pinch your nose closed with your thumb and pointer finger. Lift
your thumb and breathe in through that nostril for a count of 5.
Pinch it closed and then lift your pointer finger and breathe out
through that nostril for a count of 5. Now switch.

Download

_____
_____
_____
_____
_____
_____
_____
_____
_____
_____
_____
_____
_____
_____
_____

Dig Deep

_____
_____
_____
_____
_____
_____
_____
_____
_____
_____
_____
_____
_____

I Am Trusting

I am confident in the integrity, strength and ability of other people.

Draw

Dream

Reach out

Ask your mom, dad, or a good friend to help you let go of something bothering you.

Download

_____
_____
_____
_____
_____
_____
_____
_____
_____
_____
_____
_____
_____
_____

Dig Deep

_____
_____
_____
_____
_____
_____
_____
_____
_____
_____
_____
_____

I Am Passionate

I have strong feelings about things I believe in.

Draw

Dream

_____
_____
_____
_____
_____
_____
_____
_____
_____
_____
_____
_____
_____
_____

Play all out

Do what makes you happy and give it your all.

Download

Dig Deep

I Am Energetic

I possess a dynamic quality.

Draw

Dream

_____

_____

_____

_____

_____

_____

_____

_____

_____

_____

_____

_____

_____

_____

Do 5 Jumping Jacks

Each time yell out "I AM AWESOME!"

Download

Dig Deep

I Am Serene

I feel calm and peaceful.

Draw

Dream

_____
_____
_____
_____
_____
_____
_____
_____
_____
_____
_____
_____

Become a Butterfly

Lie down on your back. Bring the soles of your feet together and let your knees fall out to the sides. Place one hand on your belly and the other on your heart.

Download

_____
_____
_____
_____
_____
_____
_____
_____
_____
_____
_____
_____
_____
_____

Dig Deep

_____
_____
_____
_____
_____
_____
_____
_____
_____
_____
_____
_____
_____

I Am Content

I am satisfied with what I have. I don't want or need anything else.

Draw

Dream

Just Smile

Enjoy the moment.

Download

Dig Deep

I Am Beautiful

I have amazing qualities that bring great pleasure to others.

Draw

Dream

_____
_____
_____
_____
_____
_____
_____
_____
_____
_____
_____
_____
_____
_____
_____

Strike a Pose

Love yourself for who you are inside and out.

Download

Dig Deep

I Am Graceful

I bring elegance and beauty to everyday life.

Draw

Dream

_____
_____
_____
_____
_____
_____
_____
_____
_____
_____
_____
_____
_____
_____

Become a Dancer

Plant one foot on the ground. Reach for the inside of the other foot and lift your leg up as you reach your other arm forward.

Download

Dig Deep

I Am Tranquil

My mind, body and spirit are free from stress.

Draw

Dream

_____

_____

_____

_____

_____

_____

_____

_____

_____

_____

_____

_____

Let it GO

Take a deep breath in through your nose. Open your mouth and
loudly exhale out all of your air.

Download

_____
_____
_____
_____
_____
_____
_____
_____
_____
_____
_____
_____
_____
_____

Dig Deep

_____
_____
_____
_____
_____
_____
_____
_____
_____
_____
_____
_____
_____
_____

I Am Trusting

I expect others to do what they say they are going to do.

Draw

Dream

_____
_____
_____
_____
_____
_____
_____
_____
_____
_____
_____
_____
_____
_____

Sit in an imaginary chair

Have a friend stand behind you and place their legs under you so
that you are sitting on their lap. Trust that they will support you.

Download

Dig Deep

I Am Kind

This is a fundamental part of who I am. I am good natured and follow my heart.

Draw

Dream

Open your heart and mind

Lie on your stomach. Place your hands on either side of your chest like cricket wings. Press your hands into the ground and lift your heart toward the sky.

Download

Dig Deep

I Am Committed

I keep my promises.

Draw

Dream

_____
_____
_____
_____
_____
_____
_____
_____
_____
_____
_____
_____

Give yourself a Hug

Lie on your back and bring your knees to your chest. Wrap your
arms around your knees and give yourself a good squeeze.

Download

_____
_____
_____
_____
_____
_____
_____
_____
_____
_____
_____
_____
_____
_____
_____

Dig Deep

_____
_____
_____
_____
_____
_____
_____
_____
_____
_____
_____
_____
_____
_____
_____

I Am Grounded

I feel secure and comfortable in my own skin.

Draw

Dream

_____
_____
_____
_____
_____
_____
_____
_____
_____
_____
_____
_____
_____
_____

Feel safe in Child's Pose

Spread your knees wide and bring your big toes to touch. Sit
back on your heels and then reach forward placing your forehead
on the ground.

Download

Dig Deep

I Am a Friend

I am always there for the people I care about. I treat others the way I want to be treated.

Draw

Dream

_____
_____
_____
_____
_____
_____
_____
_____
_____
_____
_____
_____
_____

Surprise someone

Make someone's day by doing a random act of kindness.

Download

_____

_____

_____

_____

_____

_____

_____

_____

_____

_____

_____

_____

_____

Dig Deep

_____

_____

_____

_____

_____

_____

_____

_____

_____

_____

_____

_____

_____

I Am Secure

I am confident in everything I do.

Draw

Dream

Challenge yourself

Balance on one foot and then close your eyes.

Download

_____
_____
_____
_____
_____
_____
_____
_____
_____
_____
_____
_____
_____
_____
_____
_____

Dig Deep

_____
_____
_____
_____
_____
_____
_____
_____
_____
_____
_____
_____
_____
_____
_____

I Am Supported

I am surrounded by people who love and protect me.

Draw

Dream

_____
_____
_____
_____
_____
_____
_____
_____
_____
_____
_____
_____
_____
_____

Just Relax

Lie down on the ground and put your legs up on a wall. Feel the
support as you let your arms fall out to the sides.

Download

Dig Deep

I Am Giving

I am warm and open in relationships with other people.

Draw

Dream

_____
_____
_____
_____
_____
_____
_____
_____
_____
_____
_____
_____
_____

Reach back

Plant your feet firmly into the ground, stand up straight, and
reach your arms up to the sky. Gently bring your arms back into
a mini-backbend opening up your heart.

Download

_____
_____
_____
_____
_____
_____
_____
_____
_____
_____
_____
_____
_____
_____
_____
_____

Dig Deep

_____
_____
_____
_____
_____
_____
_____
_____
_____
_____
_____
_____
_____
_____
_____

I Am Determined

When I decide to do something I make it happen.

Draw

Dream

Feel your Core strength

Come into a high plank top of a push up position. Lift one arm and reach it forward and then lift the opposite leg and reach it back. Don't forget to do the other side.

Download

Dig Deep

I Am Able

I have the necessary power, skill and resources to accomplish anything.

Draw

Dream

_____
_____
_____
_____
_____
_____
_____
_____
_____
_____
_____
_____

Become a Downward Facing Dog

Come into a table top position with your hands spread wide like
starfish under your shoulders and your knees in line with your hips.
Tuck your toes and push back creating an inverted V with your body.

Download

Dig Deep

I Am Heard

People listen to what I have to say.

Draw

Dream

Roar like a lion

Bring your hands up like claws. Roll your eyes up to the sky, stick out your tongue, and ROAR!

Download

_____

Dig Deep

_____

I Am Communicative

I am able to express thoughts, feelings, and information easily and effectively.

Draw

Dream

_____
_____
_____
_____
_____
_____
_____
_____
_____
_____
_____
_____
_____

Make up a Song

Tell it like it is.

Download

_____
_____
_____
_____
_____
_____
_____
_____
_____
_____
_____
_____
_____
_____

Dig Deep

_____
_____
_____
_____
_____
_____
_____
_____
_____
_____
_____
_____
_____
_____

I Am Intuitive

I have the insight and ability to see the truth.

Draw

Dream

_____
_____
_____
_____
_____
_____
_____
_____
_____
_____
_____
_____
_____

Ask questions

Take time to listen to the answers.

Download

_____
_____
_____
_____
_____
_____
_____
_____
_____
_____
_____
_____
_____
_____
_____

Dig Deep

_____
_____
_____
_____
_____
_____
_____
_____
_____
_____
_____
_____
_____
_____

I Am Abundant

I experience a full life where I have it all.

Draw

Dream

_____
_____
_____
_____
_____
_____
_____
_____
_____
_____
_____
_____
_____
_____

Love your life

Take a moment to smell the roses.

Download

_____
_____
_____
_____
_____
_____
_____
_____
_____
_____
_____
_____
_____
_____
_____

Dig Deep

_____
_____
_____
_____
_____
_____
_____
_____
_____
_____
_____
_____
_____

I Am Worthy

I have great merit, character, and value.

Draw

Dream

_____
_____
_____
_____
_____
_____
_____
_____
_____
_____
_____
_____
_____

Kick up your energy

Do three karate kicks and promise yourself that you will
NEVER give up.

www.ingramcontent.com/pod-product-compliance
Lightning Source LLC
Chambersburg PA
CBHW030515100426
42813CB00001B/56

* 9 7 8 1 6 1 6 6 0 0 0 5 1 *